Write Right – Sell Now

How to Create Content That Will Grow Your Business

Matt Brennan

© 2016 Matt Brennan

MatthewLBrennan.com

"We are all apprentices in a craft where no one ever becomes a master."

- Ernest Hemmingway

Table of Contents

Forward

All of us have a story. We have all had times in our lives where we have felt pain or triumph, success or failure, silly or serious, winner or second place! It's funny how when sitting at a Starbucks or a Buffalo Wild Wings, we can express feelings and messages in very colorful and expressive ways. Then put a microphone or a keyboard in front of us, and we are reduced to a 2nd grader trying to write a term paper about Christopher Columbus or George Washington.

You have experience and a story to tell.

What's holding you back? I am not a writer? Who wants to hear what I have to say? Who cares? What's the reason? How does this help?

I felt the same way. I blogged for years, but frankly the posts sucked. I had no audience. No one paid attention, and I questioned why I was wasting my time. I know it was a way to extend my reach to new audiences, but the only people paying attention were family and friends.

I was posting about my new passion, iPhones and apps, but if 100 people paid attention a month, I felt successful. Did I have a goal? No! Did it make me money? Oh hell no! But then, what did I know? I was attracted to the format and felt it was a forum to speak to the masses of people who cared about what interested me.

Then I met Matt. He was a writer for a local suburban Chicago newspaper and a subsidiary of the Chicago Sun Times (at the time). He was not only a published author but also studied successful bloggers like Jon Morrow and Chris Brogan.

We regularly met for coffee at Starbucks and continued to build a friendship. More importantly, he encouraged me and taught me how to put a figurative USB cable in the back of my head and pull out knowledge I accumulated through years of being a corporate employee, and ultimately an entrepreneur. Those articles and blogs went from dozens of readers to ultimately millions.

Matt taught me formulas and helped me find resources about how to write headlines, how to craft stories, how to create interest throughout the writing process and more. Most important was how to create calls to actions within blogs that get results.

Blog writing can be a hobby or a business. It can be part of your marketing system, or it can become a marketing system that you can teach people and create a business from. From Matt's guidance, I learned to create profits and marketing tools I could have only imagined.

I have since written four books, three have which have been compilations from blogging. My first one was internationally award winning and an Amazon best seller! It all came from writing blogs. My second book was written as a blog for one year and turned into 101 networking tips. Matt contributed to that blog as well.

Since then he went on to do great things like become a Huffington Post published Daddy Blogger, and has taught thousands of others how he has created a success blogging that works.

I often say... If you want to learn how to make a million dollars, learn from someone who continues to make a million dollars each year (not a one hit wonder). I was in the music business and it is littered with one hit wonders!

Matt is a blogger who continues to learn and grow his audience from tens, to hundreds, to thousands, and millions! His principles are solid and I can confirm they work (they have worked for me). He continues to hone his craft (as all good writers and teachers do). Matt has a heart to teach you how and why.

If you spend an hour or two and learn only one thing, it will be time well spent, but I can assure you that there are principles, tactics, and nuggets in this book that will guide you to success as you start to navigate the jungle that is blogging.

Make no mistake, we all have more to learn and the landscape changes every day, but this book offers a solid foundation and will help you figure out where to go next.

My final piece of advice is to follow his blogs...Spiralingupwards.com and Matthewlbrennan.com. Watch what he does and model, hack, re-engineer, reverse engineer how he writes so well.

P.S. My nickname is Captain Typo. I suck at writing and my English not so good! Matt rewrote all the text on my main website and because of him, I hire people to help make that USB in the back of my head work better!

Don't let your lack of ability or fear of writing stop you from creating the audience or the business of your dreams!

Captain Typo

Brian Basilico

Author of "It's Not About You, It's About Bacon! Relationship Marketing In A Social Media World!"

Introduction

Figuring out how to market your business online can feel like paddling a rowboat into the ocean. The Internet is an overwhelmingly huge place, and your business is a tiny blip. If you're not careful, you can get lost and overpowered by the currents around you.

That's why it's best to have a plan and be intentional with your digital marketing. You need to be sure your efforts are working to bring you the new business you want. Otherwise, what you are doing may be a waste of time.

Write Right—Sell Now is about establishing the techniques you need to master, writing for your customer in the digital age. It outlines the reasons content creation is necessary, while providing practical techniques for blogging and creating web page content, in a way that will benefit those who aren't natural writers. It's a how-to guide about one of the most necessary skill sets for running a successful business in the modern economy.

Business owners should leverage any means possible to distinguish themselves from the competition. That doesn't necessarily mean being louder; it means honing your message so people stay engaged. In other words, readers are looking for valuable information. They want to learn, be entertained, and be informed.

In a crowded market, strong design helps your website and blog stick out from the competition and attract eyeballs. However, it's your content's job from that point to sell your audience members on your message and entice them to convert.

There are lots of questionable tactics out there that drive traffic to your website, but end up sacrificing your content. This traffic arrives *despite* not having a good message readily available. The problem with this approach is it doesn't drive conversions. A bad message is a bad message, whether there are dozens of people visiting your website or thousands.

It's easy to become obsessed with the amount of traffic that flows to your website, but on its own, it doesn't mean anything. You aren't paid until customers buy something. In the marketing world, traffic is a misleading metric. It does nothing to help you sell. Last time I checked, our mortgage company won't accept traffic as payment. The money that follows a conversion is what is important.

This book is designed to help you convert your strategically-earned traffic into sales. You can drive traffic to your website and compel customers to take action with a good story. I began my career as a journalist writing stories that attracted readers. Many businesses are succeeding by carrying that same practice into their content marketing. Friendly, reader-driven content will help you grow your business.

We live in an information-based economy, and your customers are going to have questions. It's in your best interest to become a resource for them. You don't have to be a natural writer to do this. Heck, you don't even have to particularly enjoy writing. As a business owner, I can tell you how much I hate accounting. But I recognize the need to do some basic bookkeeping before passing the more detailed work on to my accountant.

You will need to accept that marketing has changed and be willing to move along with the new way of doing things. You will need to put everything you have into crafting a message that your audience can identify with—that is what turns readers into customers.

You'll need to become your readers' source for industry information. That way, when they have questions, get overwhelmed, or run out of time to do things themselves, it is you they call.

In a digital economy, the business with the strongest message and best story wins. With a little research, practice, and strategic thinking, that business can easily be yours.

Chapter 1

Why Blogging and Content Creation Are a Must

Take a moment to think about your home. Close your eyes and get a good mental picture. Got it? I'm guessing you don't live in a bunker. There are doors and windows that serve as portals to the outside world.

Now, think of your website in the same context. The more portals you have to the outside world, the better. These are what keep us from feeling isolated. Think about how drab life would be without contact beyond our four walls.

With your website, the more portals to the outside world you have, the easier it is for your customers to find you. Each separate page or blog serves as an access point to your website.

Your home page is like the front door, to continue the metaphor. It's important to dress up that front door and make it look as appealing as possible. Functional design and strong marketing in that location are crucial. But why limit people to one entry point for your website, when they can come in from anywhere?

A blog offers you the chance to expand your audience by giving people multiple entry points into your house. Each post serves as a window into your website and your business. Anything you write about on the web has the potential to become the first impression a new customer has of you and your company. That makes maintaining a professional appearance crucial for expanding your audience.

A blog is also a way to improve the foundation of the house by helping you establish yourself as an expert and providing a stream of valuable content.

It keeps your business at the forefront of your audience members' minds. A good blog post keeps your readers engaged from the headline to the call to action.

Blogs, social media, and other forms of content marketing can level the playing field. They provide an avenue for businesses with smaller budgets to gain visibility. Compelling content expands your audience and increases your customer base, and it can all be created on a minimal budget.

In case you need your arm twisted a bit, here are a few quick blogging facts from marketing behemoth Hubspot:

- B2B marketers who use blogs receive **67 percent more leads** than those who do not. Those leads are available and cost nothing but your time.
- Marketers who use blogs are **13 times more likely** to enjoy a **positive return on investment**. Leads come to fruition simply by expanding the reach of your business.
- By 2020, customers will manage **85 percent** of their relationships **without talking to a human**. Customers are increasingly likely to do their own research about your

company without ever contacting you. You can control the information that is readily available through blogging.

Blogging creates the type of exposure for your business that previously was only available to companies with large marketing and advertising budgets. Thousands of people who may not have otherwise known you existed can now read your work.

Blogging is not a get-rich-quick scheme or a pathway to overnight success. But it can help grow your business and increase your bottom line. You don't have to be a naturally gifted writer, but you do need to make an effort to produce the type of content that resonates with your audience. If writing doesn't come naturally, you can read some books that will help you improve, and practice more. Or, you can hire a copywriter or copy editor to help. There are options for taking advantage of proven methods. The most important lesson is to have entertaining and informative content ready for your audience.

Chapter 2

Imagination and Focus

Bring a Little Imagination to What You Do

There are probably many people out there who do what you do, no matter what industry you are in. With digital marketing, they are communicating their message to new audiences in similar ways.

When the crowd veers right at the fork in the road, it may be time for you to hang a left. It's more important now than ever to remember that there are multiple ways of doing things, and you don't have to stay stuck in the patterns you witness other places.

It's time to use some imagination. I am always looking for outside inspiration. Luckily, I rarely have to look further than my everyday life.

I spend the majority of my days surrounded by three-year-olds. My son and my dog are within a month of age, and both teach compelling lessons when it comes to life and business.

Watching the imagination of a toddler at work can be a great reminder on the importance of creativity.

I try to spend my evenings playing with my son. He recently invited me to sail out with him on his pirate ship, which coincidentally doubles as a fantastic cedar chest.

For a moment we were father-and-son pirates, sailing the open sea without leaving the living room. We sang that old pirate favorite, "Jingle Bells," at my son's persistent request.

No matter how ingrained you are in your industry, you can be the fresh set of eyes willing to do things a little differently. Sure, I can scoff at a three-year-old and tell him how ridiculous it would be to sit on a cedar chest singing "Jingle Bells" months after Christmas. But why would I? He's got such a vivid imagination, and it's beautiful. I don't care who you are, when a three-year-old tells you to hop on his pirate ship and sing with him, it's all hands on deck.

It's time to view your marketing materials in a new light; to see what they could be.

Companies such as American Science and Surplus, Trader Joe's, and The Dollar Shave Club all provide a terrifically fresh approach to their content and messaging. Seriously, Google any of them and you'll be in for some entertaining reading.

Are you doing what you can to make your marketing materials original? Are you considering your industry, and your subject matter from all angles? Don't take your writing too seriously. That three-year-old is calling you to sit on his pirate ship and sing "Jingle Bells." Are you listening?

Stay Focused

Any time you get on the computer, there are a thousand digital distractions. Facebook and Twitter beckon your attention, posts and comments need to be responded to, and e-mails flood your inbox. You can try justifying that responding to some of this is actually helping your marketing plans.

But is it *really* what you need to be doing at the time? Maybe it is, maybe it's not. The reality is that you should have a marketing plan and goals, and each action you take should bring you closer to those goals. Like with imagination, I don't have to look far to find my inspiration for focus.

My family and I adopted an 80-pound German shepherd/hound mix named Captain last summer. When we brought him home, he showed a few signs of separation anxiety. The previous owner also gave us a few clues indicating that anxiety could be an issue.

We knew we couldn't stay home every minute of every day with our new family member, so we devised a plan. We crated him inside our laundry room thinking that would take care of the problem. I left the house for a few hours to work. When I returned, Captain greeted me at the front door.

I knew I had a problem. I followed our four-legged escape artist back to the scene of the crime. He freed the door on the crate without doing any damage to the crate or himself. Even more impressive was that he managed to claw and chew his way through my laundry room door in the short time I was away, leaving piles of wood shards scattered about. Luckily, he managed this without getting any splinters in his mouth or paws.

The door that once kept Captain contained, now had a German-shepherd-shaped hole on the right side. Nothing else in the basement was damaged that afternoon. He simply wanted out—he had a singular focus.

Captain remained obsessed with escaping confinement. Nothing in his physical environment distracted him from the importance of this mission. He wanted to be in the company of his new owners in the shortest amount of time possible.

I learned three valuable lessons from this initial episode with Captain:

1. Hollow core doors suck.

2. It takes a whole lot of blind trust (or stupidity) to give a destructive, uncratable dog free reign of the house.

3. A key aspect of achieving results is maintaining focus.

As business owners, it is important to maintain focus. Otherwise, we become distracted by unnecessary noise. We may be able to convince ourselves that our business is better as a result of our social media or e-mail obsessions, but not if our time there is unfocused and not aimed at meeting our larger business goals.

There is likely a larger goal that requires more focus. It's important to have a plan to complete the truly meaningful tasks that advance our businesses, and stick with it. You should know what those tasks are, and filter out the background noise. Understand your big-picture goals, and make sure that everything you do within your content marketing works toward those goals.

Captain has become my new shining example of focus. He is a specialist with a lot of talent. He has gotten off his leash in the past and quickly found his way home. I wish I were as good at anything as Captain is at seeking the company of his people.

As business owners, we need to stay focused on our marketing plans and finding the solutions to grow our business. How much time are you spending working on advancing your business, and how much are you caving to your distractions?

Can you muster up the same singularity of focus as a dog on a mission?

Chapter 3

What Makes You Different?

One of the simultaneously best and worst things about digital marketing is that it takes geography out of the equation when it comes to expanding your customer base. Unless you provide a localized service, your spot on the map no longer matters in terms of your reach.

How can this be both good and bad? Obviously, it is a good thing because it expands your readership. You can market your business to anyone worldwide who may be interested in your services.

The downside is that your business now has significantly more competition. It can be tough to distinguish yourself from the others that appear in the search results, on social media, or wherever your customer might have found you.

Overcoming this requires having a keen understanding of your business. What makes you different? Why should your customers buy from you? You may offer many of the same services as other online competitors, so there has to be something different with your services, your product, or your experience that helps you stand out. This becomes your unique selling point.

Find something you do different from the competition and highlight it. There is something in the newspaper world called pack journalism. It is the idea of writing the same story that every other paper wrote, mainly because every other paper wrote it. This happens because journalists and editors don't want to answer to their higher-ups or their readers when it comes to missing out on a story. Businesses can easily fall into the same trap as they write their marketing materials.

Fight the temptation to do everything your competition does, as you produce content. Find ways to separate yourself from the pack. It will serve you better in the long run. A fresh approach is necessary for your audience to take notice of what you offer.

Chapter 4

Focusing on Your Reader

As a business owner and an industry expert, you have a great amount of knowledge, which becomes a key asset as you focus on becoming a resource for your customers and clients. How you go about communicating your expertise will go a long way in determining your success.

It's easy to forget that your customers may not have the extensive background in your field that you do. It's also easy to assume your readers know more than they do, which can lead to a knowledge gap. What does this look like as it's practiced?

Maybe you throw in phrases your reader won't understand. You may communicate ideas that make more sense in an industry journal than a communication to your customers. All of this can lead to a disengaged reader.

Keeping your readers interested requires a simple adjustment to your mindset as you establish your marketing materials. Who are you trying to sell to? I know it's tempting to answer, "Anyone who will buy." But a general answer like that doesn't help you in your endeavors.

When you understand that you are trying to reach career-minded, college-graduate men between the ages of 30 and 45 with an average income of six figures, you can target your messages to the social media platforms the people in this demographic are most likely to use, the blogs they are likely to read, and the consumer goods they are most likely to be interested in. This helps you communicate in a way that resonates with your specific customers.

It can be helpful to come up with a profile for your target customer that includes career, family status, age, home, or any other specific information that may give you an indication of how to talk with them.

The most successful business owners are able to put themselves in someone else's shoes, communicate to that person's needs, and convince their audience they offer the right solutions.

Building a successful business is not about you and how much you can sell. It's about your reader and matching up what you offer to their needs. Your readers only give you a few seconds to see if your blog post or online content matches up with what they are looking for. It's a small window and you have to do everything possible to keep it open.

Healing Your Customers' Pain

Your main purpose in business is to heal your customers' pain—to solve their problem. This is a key concept to keep in mind as you develop website content, a blogging strategy, general public relations, and brand messaging in the digital age.

What are the questions your customers continually ask? How does your product or service make your customers' lives better? Your customers are conducting web searches right now to find out more about your industry. Are you the best-positioned business as the remedy to their pain point?

Keep this idea in mind as you blog. Make sure you understand what your readers are looking for so that you are marketing *to* them instead of *at* them. Nobody voluntarily spends his or her day reading ads. Potential customers are looking for an informative take on the industry or product.

You strengthen your business's position when you are seen as the solution to the problem. When you produce marketing that holds value to the reader, it can become a valuable asset for your business.

Every blog and every page on your website should meet your readers' needs in some way.

Chapter 5

Choosing the Right Words

I recently listened to a podcast with marketing mogul Seth Godin as the guest. Godin talked about his fascination with making the perfect cup of coffee even though he doesn't drink it himself. He simply enjoyed his time perfecting the craft.

It begins with roasting your own beans, he said. The reason for roasting your own beans is simple. You maintain complete control over the cup this way. It's going to be awfully tough to make the perfect cup of coffee when you are working with substandard ingredients.

Maintaining control over the ingredients is useful outside the kitchen as well. For example, quality gardening requires attention paid to sun, watering, and soil conditions. It requires understanding the needs of each plant. Quality woodworking is another example; you need to know the intricacies of the raw materials.

Quality writing requires a heavy attention to word choice. Spending a considerable amount of time choosing the right word can feel overwhelming and tedious. But it is important, because it is what your reader will remember.

There are certain psychological keywords that have been proven to help you write to sell. The popular content marketing blog Copyblogger highlights five words as the most persuasive words in the English language: you, free, because, instantly, and new.

You: This is a connecting word that helps establish a rapport with your readers. They feel like you are addressing them directly. "You" is a great word to work into your copy whenever possible.

Free: Giving something valuable away for free is a great way to grab attention. The word "free" is a trigger. Customers are inclined to give whatever you are offering a try simply because there is no risk to them.

Because: Your readers have one pressing question: "What's in it for me?" The word "because" serves as a clue that you are about to answer that question. Make sure whatever follows this phrase is loaded with value.

Instantly: Fast results sell themselves. Which blog post would you rather read?

How to Lose 20 Pounds in Six Weeks or *How to Lose 20 Pounds*? The promise of speedy results is enough to draw people in.

New: The word "new" is an indication you are about to do something different, and a lot of times different can mean better. Using "new" in your writing can help you stick out from the pack. It can be a great way to increase value.

Advertising mogul David Ogilvy had his own list of impactful words that can help you sell. Ogilvy thrived during the era of print advertising, and his list is still relevant today. If you want to have a little fun, picture yourself watching an infomercial at two o'clock in the morning as you read this list. Be ready to pull out your credit card and buy something:

Suddenly	Revolutionary
Miracle	Quick
Now	Hurry
Announcing	Bargain
Introducing	Compare
Improvement	Challenge
Amazing	Remarkable
Sensational	Wanted
Magic	Easy
Offer	Startling

These words help convince the reader of your merit. They help you identify with the readers' problem and present your product or service as the solution.

Take a look at your previous content and consider sprinkling some of these words in, where applicable. Use them in

upcoming content.

Next time you feel compelled to buy

something online, pay attention to the

messaging used in the company's copy.

Do any of these words appear? What

other words or phrases did they use that

convinced you to buy? Consider jotting

these words down in a notebook and

using them whenever possible.

Like creating the perfect cup of coffee,

writing an effective blog post requires

meticulous attention to the details.

Chapter 6

Understanding How Features Are Different from Benefits

When was the last time you bought a computer or a car? What kind of information did the salesperson give you?

Did your computer rep try to convince you of how many gigs of RAM you need? Or did he or she ask you what you primarily use your computer for? If you're anything like me or most of the general computing public, you don't care about how much RAM you have. But you do care how fast your computer works.

You care about surfing the web with multiple tabs open while you write a Word document or edit pictures. Maybe you want the ability to play some music in the background as you do this.

A segment of car enthusiasts is going to drool over the prospect of a V-8 engine. The rest of us will simply like the idea of being able to climb from zero to 60 miles per hour in just a few seconds. So make sure you state the benefits in a way that resonates with your key audience.

Features are the technical specs for a product (RAM, V-8 engine). Benefits are how those features translate into helping the customer. You may have a loyalist crowd within your industry that understands and compares product features. But chances are the majority of your customers are going to care more about benefits and how your product solves their problem.

We all like to consider ourselves logical beings, but the truth is we often buy based on emotion. Benefits give your readers a glimpse at how you make their lives better. They make the reader feel good about buying your product. So whenever possible, make sure you are painting a picture with benefits in your writing.

Chapter 7

Story, and Why It Is Crucial

Most people don't have a photographic memory. They can't remember what they did on this day last year or what the weather was like on October 2, 1992. They'll only remember specific details if something significant happened. I know I can't recall events from either of these days.

Do you know what people do remember? Stories. My guess is you remember more details about the day you attended a family wedding, or where you were for

major historical events, such as Sept.
11, 2001. If you think long enough, you
probably have an example of an odd
factoid you picked up somewhere, and
you remember it because it was
conveyed as part of a unique story.

When we evoke an emotional response
by telling compelling stories, people pay
attention. It's time to tell some great
stories about your industry, business, or
customers. This helps the details of your
business sink in with your audience.

Here are some situations that may call
for a good story:

- Sharing how a customer used your product to solve his or her problem
- Talking about how your business started
- Educating your clients on a current industry or news story

All of these make for excellent blog posts, but don't stop there. You can also use simple writing tricks to tell better stories, making your message feel friendlier and more relatable. These techniques help you draw your customers into what you have to say:

Show, Don't Tell

Let's say you're a personal trainer

looking to tell the story of a client at the beginning of his weight loss journey. That story could start one of two ways.

Option 1

John woke up every morning at 5:30 a.m. for the last three years. The last thing he wanted to do was set the alarm clock even earlier to go work out— especially with a toddler in the house who guaranteed a night of interrupted sleep.

Tired and frustrated, with little time to exercise, John continued to eat, remained stressed out, and packed on a few pounds. That is until he made a

commitment to change.

Option 2

John was tired, stressed, and liked to

eat.

We learn a heck of a lot more about John in option 1. He becomes a more memorable character who many of us can sympathize with and relate with. If the story continues to talk about John's weight loss (as it likely would), he becomes someone we would all like to emulate.

Write How You Talk

Your mother knows you are smart. She's already proud. Your customers don't really care, though. So you can stop trying to convey your intelligence with high-level vocabulary words at every turn.

A blog post shouldn't read like an academic dissertation, or be chock-full of acronyms. If you find that you have to include new concepts, make sure you explain them for your readers.

Keep your ideal customers in mind. They probably don't know what you know about your industry, so you'll need to meet them where they're at.

Picture yourself out for coffee with a customer or client. Write in a way that is helpful to that person. Ditch the geek speak and talk with the person who's right there and interested. Your readers are real people. Even though you can't see them as they read your marketing, you have to relate.

Write Conversationally

Continue picturing yourself at coffee with your ideal reader or customer. When you talk, do you draw out every word that could otherwise be used in a contraction? Probably not. It's too formal for a conversational setting. The same applies with your marketing writing.

Avoiding contractions can make you sound stuffy. In an effort to be professional, you could be writing in a way that is disconnected. Apostrophes aren't the devil, so don't be afraid to use them. Just be sure your copy doesn't sound like your teenager's text messages.

Tell an Anecdote Here and There

Your writing should not feel stale and scripted. If there is an anecdote that bolsters your point, tell it. In fact, anecdotes are a great way to show, and not tell. They give your writing a much more personable flair and allow others to identify with you. If you use them, make certain they serve your larger point and don't take the reader on an unnecessary tangent.

Stay on Topic

You may have a fantastic anecdote or a point that makes sense. But ask yourself what the central message is. Does what you are writing support your main argument? If not, hit delete. Maybe you're writing the best paragraph you've ever written, but if it doesn't support your main argument, you guessed it, you don't need it.

If you can't live without it, put it in a new Word document and leave it there. It may be a great piece for another blog post.

Read Your Post Out Loud

This is a great editing technique that can help you catch mistakes you might have otherwise let slip. It also forces you to concentrate on the tone and helps you pay attention to how others may read it.

You may realize you used the same word three times in two sentences, or that people need to take multiple breaths while reading one sentence. There are a number of things that become noticeable when you read your work out loud before publishing.

All of these techniques can give your writing a more narrative feel, and help you tell a better story. They work wonders to strengthen your writing and make it something your audience can identify with. The better you become at these techniques, the stronger your message will be.

Chapter 8

Building Value

Your readers must perceive value in what you offer to be convinced to pull out their wallets and make a purchase. That means you'll want to show them exactly why they need what you sell and how they'll benefit from the deal.

Testimonials and case studies help convey your value. These opportunities show a third-party validation for the work you do. You can talk about how great your business, service, or product is until you're blue in the face. However, the minute someone else speaks on your behalf, the value of your business becomes much more believable and people begin to open up to your service. A testimonial carries a lot of weight with your customers. There is more on this topic later in the book.

Another aspect of building value is talking about your products and services in a way that resonates with your readers and addresses their concerns. Show your customers exactly how effective your product is at solving their problem. Video or pictures can also be a good way to convey the effectiveness of a product.

Ask yourself what the cost will be to your customer if he or she doesn't use your product. Think about it this way. If you are experiencing a toothache, there isn't much incentive to delay going to a dentist. The pain (and financial cost) might be greater a month from now than it is today. The value is in the immediate use of your product or services.

How are you conveying that in your content?

Chapter 9

Developing a Distinctive Voice

There's a lot of material out there about developing your writing voice. It has a lot to do with being authentic, and writing something that resonates with your readers, but what does that even mean?

When most people think of voice, they think of actors, singers, public speakers, podcasters, or anyone making a living through an audible voice. Your writing voice isn't the same thing.

When it comes to writing, voice refers to your style and message. Are you writing in a way that truly reflects your business? Are you writing how you would talk? Your writing should take on some of your personality—that is your writing voice. In a world where so many businesses are producing the same type of content, injecting your voice into your work sets you apart from the others.

If you are in a business that requires in-person or telephone contact with customers, there is a certain voice that you will use with your customers. You want to be friendly, knowledgeable, genuine, and authentic.

The same should be true in any website or content marketing copy. You'll want to maintain that same friendly tone that you would use if you were talking in person with your customers.

Developing your voice can draw people into your writing, giving it more personality. It can be the difference between readers continuing on your site and moving on to the next of many search results.

Chapter 10

Writing Informative Copy

No one goes on the Internet with the hope of being sold to. Instead, they go online seeking information and resources to make the purchasing process easier. They want to know:

- How to solve their particular problem
- How to navigate the purchasing process within your industry
- How to become a well-informed consumer

- How your product is the solution they are looking for
- How to complete a project themselves

Your blog is a great place to speak to potential customers who may not be ready to buy but, instead, are in a research phase. As you are talking with customers face-to-face, consider the questions they most frequently ask. Are there resources within your industry you are consistently referring your customers to? Your blog may be the perfect place to address frequent customer needs, and establish yourself as a primary resource.

It may seem counterintuitive, but businesses should be giving away as much information as possible through their blogs. That information becomes invaluable to the consumer, and you become a resource. There are aspects of your industry that seem like common sense to you but provide a challenge for your customer. Even though you give away the method for completing your process, they may likely want your assistance down the road.

Let's take the example of a plumber. He or she might have posts on "How to fix a leaky sink," or "How to keep your drains clean." The do-it-yourself crowd will find this information helpful. But there are lots of people (including me) who might get a few steps in to this undertaking, feel overwhelmed, and gladly decide to pay someone for the service because they recognize the value. The person who will most likely jump to mind to provide the service is the person who wrote the blog post.

Once this material is posted on your blog, it can be used as a resource in multiple ways. For example, you could print paper copies for in-person client education. You could package them in a client newsletter. There are creative ways to give older posts additional life and build your credibility as a resource.

As you blog and produce content for your website, it is important to be helpful, and provide your readers with as much information as you can.

Chapter 11

The Best Possible Headline

Your headline is the single largest factor determining whether someone reads your website content or blog post. Considering the average Internet user has the attention span of a gnat, your headline needs to be direct.

The average Internet user will find your post in one of two ways:

- **A social newsfeed or stream:** There are hundreds of options vying for a reader's attention in his or her social streams and news feeds. Your headline is what jumps up and down screaming, "Pick me!" Don't let this be a repeat of gym class basketball. Your online efforts won't amount to much if you go unpicked.

- **A search results page:** Your headline needs to be compelling enough to stand out on a search results page. You'll be up against 10 other listings on that page and potentially hundreds or thousands in total.

Headlines are the shortest part of the post. It's tempting to skimp on them and treat them like an afterthought. But given that they play such an important role in your communications, you need to give them more attention if you want readers to focus on you.

A lot of thought and care went into your message. You want people to read your headline and follow through with the rest of your content. These five headline tips can expand your audience:

- **Make (and keep) alluring promises:** What do you want to accomplish with your post? What does the reader who makes it to the last word walk away with? Tell people up front and be as specific as possible. Don't just tell your readers that they'll lose weight (there are hundreds of weight loss articles out there). Tell them they'll be able to do it in an easy way that they've never thought of before. They're busy people. Tell them that something they previously thought of as difficult isn't nearly as hard as they think it is. Then deliver.

- **State the benefit:** Here's the bottom line—your readers are a selfish bunch. Don't judge them for it. They have a lot of options for information. If your piece doesn't immediately meet their needs, they will move on. What can you do about this? Make sure that your headline answers the basic question on everyone's mind: "What's in it for me?" Make sure your readers understand what kind of benefit they'll receive from the investment of reading your content.

- **Use the power of numbers:** Lists are psychological crack for readers. They don't just find out how to accomplish something new, they do it in five easy steps. Headlines that offer that numeral up front tend to perform better. They're specific about what the reader can expect to take away from the experience. They make something that previously seemed difficult or complicated much easier.

- **Use provoking adjectives:** You have limited space when you're writing an attention-grabbing headline. Make sure that you're using words that draw people in. Your readers depend on you to be the expert and relay information in a digestible manner. Your headline should relax reader expectations of your subject matter. Here are some adjectives that can help you accomplish that: effortless, fun, exciting, strange, free, easy, different, and essential. Next time you are going through the grocery line, think about why you want to pick up one of the tabloid magazines and read.

- **Break away from the routine:** Variety is key in any type of marketing; headline writing is no different. You'll need to find multiple ways to connect with your audience to consistently hold its attention. It's important to avoid predictability. Don't write all your blog posts as lists or always lead in with annoying click bait "You'll Never Guess What Happens Next" headlines. Vary your technique to keep your readers interested.

There is so much information out there about writing a great headline. Consider reading Jon Morrow's *Headline Hacks*, which is available for free online, or David Garfinkel's *Headlines That Make You Rich* for some all-inclusive advice on becoming a headline-writing machine.

Spend some time practicing this skill. Don't be afraid to spend a disproportionate amount of time on those few words atop the page. The rewards to your business can be

astounding.

Chapter 12

Engage Your Reader

In journalism, the first sentence of a news story is called the lead. The job of the lead is to draw people into your content and make them keep reading. Sentence by sentence, you want to create a story that they can't put down.

Journalists know this goal isn't reachable by simply reciting the facts. You also won't create engaging marketing content by being overly promotional. Today's potential customers are seeking out information, not a commercial. They understand the difference.

Remember, telling stories and giving your writing a more narrative flair are great ways to hook your audience. There's a newsroom cliché, that people love to read about people. If your business has stories about how your product made your customers' lives better, tell them. Stories give your readers an emotional hook. They give people something they can identify with, allowing them to feel a bond with you. They can make your business stronger in a way that simply reciting data or talking points never will.

Engaging people with your content also requires strong verbs and tight writing. It requires using an online thesaurus when your stale word choice would bore your most caffeinated readers to sleep. It involves making sure you're not overusing filler words. Here are a few filler words that don't add anything to your message. When these creep into your copy, you can usually delete them:

- In order
- Just
- Literally
- Quite
- Really
- Very

These words fail to provide any additional insight. For example, if something is "very helpful," it can more simply be described as "helpful." Instead of writing "I just want to read," you can write "I want to read," and get your same point across.

Eliminating unnecessary words trims the fat out of your writing and helps keep your reader engaged.

Chapter 13

Using Testimonials

You can stand up in the middle of a room and shout about how great your company is. If you're talking to the right audience, maybe people will listen. Maybe they won't. You can explain your greatness with prolific stories and ideas and have the data to back up every last piece of them. Maybe people will listen. Maybe they won't.

Do you know what stands out and makes the greatest difference to your readers? When other people stand up and shout your praises. There is a lot more weight behind happy customers talking about how great you are to work with and how quickly you solved their problems than there is behind you tooting your own horn. That's just how the world works. It's similar to an Amazon review. Third-party opinion will always be important.

This means a few things for your business. First, you should always be asking customers about their experience as you work with them—it's just good customer service. Assuming you are good at what you do, you might even get something nice to use as a testimonial.

Next, these testimonials can be used in a variety of ways. You can start by asking someone to provide a LinkedIn recommendation. The recommendations go a long way toward improving your professional profile. Once you have a LinkedIn recommendation, you can copy and paste that to your website, for additional social proof.

Many businesses set up a testimonials page. Another strategy is to use a testimonial on the bottom of your site's main pages so people's thoughts about your company appear in prominent site locations. Other people's positive experiences with your company are then heavily featured where your readers can easily see them.

This can validate you in your readers' eyes. Third-party testimonials show people that you can be trusted to help them and solve their problem.

Chapter 14

A Call to Action and Why You Need One

You may be an excellent writer who is completely capable of writing educational, informative, entertaining copy that moves your reader. But here's the thing: that alone is not enough. As a business owner, it's a dangerous risk to assume that your readers know what you want them to do. Whether you are writing website content, blogs, brochures, or any other type of marketing or sales copy, you'll want to tell your readers exactly what you want them to do.

Your writing doesn't always have to ask for a sale (though sometimes it should). Your blogs for instance can ask for comments, shares, e-mail addresses, e-book downloads, or any other activity you are looking for your readers to engage in.

Blogs can be slightly murkier ground when it comes to calls to action, because they are supposed to serve a more informal educational purpose. You are in business, however, and it is OK to ask for a sale from time to time. If you've done your job in providing useful information that readers value, they shouldn't mind if you use a sentence or two to ask for the sale at the end of a 600-word blog post.

As a journalist, my goal was always to create a story that someone would clip from the paper and save the refrigerator. I wanted to write pieces that had meaning. It wasn't enough to write about a fundraiser, I needed to provide the 5W's (who, what, when, where, why) and remind people how they could get involved.

It's no different here. Make sure you tell the whole story while providing meaning and value to your reader. If you stir up the right emotions in people, they will be more likely to follow through when you tell them how to take action.

Chapter 15

Long Copy Versus Short Copy

One of the most frequent questions business owners who are new to the web or blogging ask is about the length of the copy they should be producing. This is going to depend on several factors:

- Are you selling cars or packs of bubble gum? The more complicated the product you are selling is, the more copy it might take to educate your clients.
- Are you trying to rank your website and blog within the search

engines? (There's more on search engine optimization in the next chapter.) Google typically only ranks content of about 300 words or longer. There are several other ranking factors, but it's a good idea for your website copy and blogs to be at least this long if you are serious about being found.

- Do you tell the whole story? I worked with a newspaper editor who told reporters to let the story dictate the length. If you set out to explain a complicated concept, what you write could be longer than your average post length— and that's OK. Don't skimp on the details simply to shorten the content. Conversely, don't overwrite and bog us down in detail we don't need.

I've seen blog posts reach upward of 2,000 words. And you know what? I didn't even realize it was that long when I was reading it because it was packed with great information. I've also seen some amazingly profound posts come in between 50 and 200 words.

If you are going to write long, make sure you're writing about a story or subject that your readers care deeply about. Also, it should be on a subject that warrants that kind of length. You'll also want to spend extra time making sure the writing is of a higher quality to keep your readers interested from beginning to end.

Think visually when writing long. Below is a list of a few different ways you can break up long blocks of text to make them easier for your reader to finish. Use:

- Multiple photographs or graphics
- Subheadings
- Lists
- Shorter paragraphs
- Infographics

Consider your subject matter and don't be afraid to vary the length of your posts. You may find that you pick up new readers as you try different approaches.

Chapter 16

What's the Role of SEO?

SEO stands for search engine optimization and is just fancy speak for making your website findable in search engines.

Keywords and key phrases are a central component of SEO and they can lead your potential customer to you based on what he or she enters into the search engine.

What phrase do you want to rank for when your potential customer types it into the search engine? There are entire websites and books devoted to SEO, but I will give you a cursory overview to help you understand the basics of the issue. Each website page and each blog post can rank for specific keywords used on that page. It's important to consider exactly what you want your website to rank for as you write your content.

1. Go to Google's Keyword Planner and sign in using your Google account.

2. Click the first option, **Search for new keywords using a phrase, website or category**. If you were an accountant writing about tax

season, you'd type "tax season"
into the field for your product or
service.

3. Click **keyword ideas**. You'll see a
table of useful information.

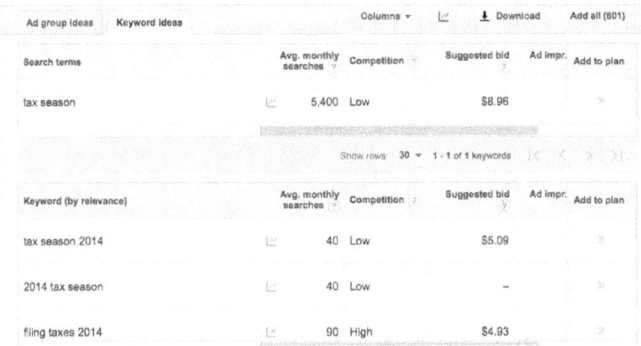

The table shows that there were 5,400
average monthly searches for this phrase
with a low competition level. This is
good. It means there is a high search
volume and not a lot of people trying to
rank for this particular phrase. (The

suggested bid category is beyond the scope of this book.)

Below the tax season information is a table with suggested phrases. This information becomes incredibly useful because you will find other keyword options with the same ranking information. Many times the term you initially want to rank for has better alternatives listed in the table.

The goal is to pick a phrase that can naturally be worked into the content you are trying to produce, and use it a handful of times. You'll want to use it within the content somewhere between a

0.5 percent and 2.5 percent density, throughout the entire written piece. The keyword density is how often throughout the piece the keyword is being used. SEO plugins on WordPress (or even a calculator) can help you figure out your numbers.

One last note on keywords—they shouldn't come at the expense of your reader. Avoid inundating your copy with them simply to rank in the search engines. This only distracts your reader. Generally you can be successful by picking a natural keyword that makes sense then flowing it into the copy a handful of times. Remember, you are trying to motivate your reader to pull out a credit card or to call you.

SEO is a large, expansive subject that constantly changes. I would encourage you to Google "Search Engine Optimization" and find out as much information as you can. Some other great resources include:

- Moz (Moz.com)
- Copyblogger (Copyblogger.com)
- Search Engine Journal (Searchenginejournal.com)
- Search Engine Land (Searchengineland.com)

Chapter 17

Why Spelling and Grammar Count

It's the digital age—every word can be abbreviated, and punctuation is optional. E-mails, texts, and social media updates are havens for bad grammar and spelling.

Maybe you don't like writing much and never put much effort into the basics. But here's the thing: in every piece of writing that you do for your business, you are out to build credibility. That piece of writing you are zipping through to move on to the next project may be what creates the first impression of your business for a prospective customer.

When your writing is filled with grammar mistakes or misspellings, it creates stopping points and makes readers question your professionalism—neither will do your business any favors.

Your writing can and should be conversational and informal, but as long as you are representing your business and looking to expand your audience, it should also be professional.

You'll want to use spell-check every time you publish anything. But don't stop there. Next I'll share some tips to edit

your work so that mistakes that cause

natural stopping points for your readers

don't creep into your work.

Chapter 18

Tips for Editing Your Work

Writing is a creative process and becoming critical of your work before your message has hit the paper can cripple your output. As a writer, it is easy to get in the way of your own ideas. That's why it's best to purge all your ideas onto the page in draft form and mold them from there.

Book editors often do a read through looking for structural, thematic, and big-picture writing issues. They edit for story and structure. This may mean omitting sentences or paragraphs that do not support the ideas or themes you are trying to convey. Many editors will try to pare the document by about 10 percent. You can do the same thing to help your writing. No matter what, the goal is to produce a clear and concise document you can be proud of.

Hiring a copy editor greatly improves the quality of your work. It helps ensure your published work is of the highest professional quality. I hired a copy editor to help edit the content of this book. She fixed a lot of grammatical errors and offered a lot of conceptual changes I ended up using. I'd highly recommend this route for anyone thinking of writing their own business marketing content.

If you don't want to pay a copywriter or editor, you can ask someone close to you to read your work before you publish.

When we write, we become particularly close to the subject and attached to our work. We have been through our own writing multiple times, and our brains may gloss over a simple mistake that a fresh set of eyes could catch right away. Having someone new look over your material can greatly improve the quality of your work.

Chapter 19

Publishing Only the Best

That little publish button jumps out at you on WordPress. It sits right there, begging for attention. Here's the thing. Decades ago, there would be a gatekeeper at whatever newspaper, magazine, or other medium you were lucky enough to have your work published in. Chances are that he or she would be fairly selective in the publication process.

The result of that professional choosiness was that only the best writing would be published. Second-tier work sat unloved with no audience, and there were few alternative channels for it.

Publishing doesn't work that way anymore. With your website and blog, you can get your writing in front of a much broader audience, and there is no longer a gatekeeper to dictate what is or isn't published. That doesn't mean it's time to relax, however.

By now you should understand that anything you write or post can form a reader's opinion about your business. Even though it's tempting to slap a headline on your blog post, forgo any rereads or editing, and hit publish to be done with it, you'll want to put more care into your writing in the long run.

Below is a checklist I use and provide clients. You should be able to say that you've done the majority of these things before you publish your writing (or at least have a good reason why you haven't done them).

Before you publish, have you:

- √ Thought about who your audience is, and what their level of knowledge is about the subject matter?

- √ Defined industry terminology to a level that your readers or customers will understand?

- √ Written a headline that engages the reader?

√ Used Google's Keyword Planner tool to determine the best keyword phrases for a search?

√ Read your content out loud?

√ Included a call to action so that your readers know what you want them to do?

√ Run spell-check?

√ Determined that you used the right version of it's/its, their/they're/there, your/you're, or any other word with multiple spellings?

√ Asked someone else to read your work for input?

√ Found a good photo to accompany your writing?

Chapter 20

How You Can Use the Information in This Book

One of the most frustrating things about marketing and business books is that many give you a lot of information but no real practical methods for using it. I hope that you can take some of the strategies discussed and implement them to better connect with your audience, and see more success with your business's calls to action.

In case you are still wondering how to use some of the information in this book, here's an overview to help you write to sell.

Develop your website copy: Your website is the "home base" for all of your marketing efforts. It's your little space on the Internet where any information you want to share about your company goes. You're not subject to any social media platform's terms of service here, so you are free to publish anything when and how you see fit.

Establish your customers' pain point: What are your customers struggling with? How are you best equipped to help them? What do you sell that makes their life a little easier? Make sure you have answers to all these questions. As your readers find you through search or social media, they are going to want quick answers to this. The higher up the page you can show them that you understand their problem, and you are the right person to solve it, the better.

Don't fall into the trap of simply listing what you sell and the features involved. Instead, show your readers how they will benefit.

Write website content aimed at your customers: Show your customers not only that you understand their pain, but also that you are their best option for healing it. What do you do that no one else can? What experience do you bring to the table that differentiates you from the competition? Remember, your reader is busy and has plenty of other options. They've chosen to learn more about your business. Make sure you give them what they are looking for.

Let your readers know how to find you: Don't make it hard for them to reach you. Is your contact information readily available? Have you told them exactly how to be in touch? If you want your readers to engage with you through Facebook, LinkedIn, Twitter, or any of your other social media channels, make sure you've let them know. For instance, my email is readily available on my website, and in my "About the Author" section for this book. Feel free to say hi!

Tell a compelling story: It doesn't matter how great your product is if you cannot keep your audience interested. Remember, great design draws eyeballs in, and a compelling story is what moves them to act. Your readers will remember a story long after they forget any statistics you use to quote the effectiveness of your product. The emotion evoked by a great story is one of the most effective sales tools you could possibly ask for.

Use an authentic voice: Your competition is likely writing about some of the same information you are. A distinct and authentic voice is one of your best assets as you work to differentiate your business. Write your marketing copy in the same voice you would use to talk with your customers. Are you normally sarcastic, funny, or less than formal? That's OK! Writing your marketing materials in the same voice is a genuine move. It makes you a little more fun and likeable. Remember, professional business writing can still be fun. Use a voice that is appropriate for your business, but you don't *have* to sound like you are writing a dissertation paper.

Integrate your marketing efforts:
Your website should be letting your customers know about your storefront, social channels, offline materials, and any other way that your customers can find you. Your offline materials and social media channels should be letting your customers know about your website. Give your audience an incentive for finding your business in a new location. Discounts for an online review or Facebook interaction may help generate

buzz around your business. Think about new ways to use brochures, postcards, and other offline tools to bring people into the digital fold. The more contact customers have with your business, the better.

Publish professional marketing materials: Is your marketing material representing you in the most professional light? An informal voice is OK, but taking shortcuts on things like grammar and spelling is not. Make sure you are using the right version of words like their, they're, and there, and it's and its. Always run spell-check and ensure that your writing is as mistake free as possible. While errors may not matter much to you, they matter to your audience. Simple mistakes can erode your customers' trust in what you do and could easily cost you a sale, or long term business.

Hire a copywriter: We all have our least favorite aspects of running a business. Maybe it's our least favorite because it's not how we want to spend our time, or maybe it's because we flat out suck at it. I didn't become a freelance writer because I excel in accounting. Believe me; I am very grateful to my accountant around tax time. There's no shame in outsourcing work. Strong writing and

communications are essential to any

business in today's world. You can hire a

copywriter and come out the other end

with a better product.

Conclusion

By now you should understand the importance of strong writing skills in business. Whether you are writing for your website, social media, or another marketing channel, understanding how to engage your audience with compelling content is a necessary skill for any business owner or entrepreneur.

Remember, your marketing needs to be about addressing your audience's needs. Your headlines are arguably the most important piece of your writing because they are what your reader bases the decision to continue reading on. From there, it is about the quality of the content, telling a good story, and moving your reader to act.

Design draws people into your website. It makes for a friendlier experience. But it is the content that causes the reader to close the browser window before completing your call to action.

So show your readers you understand their pain point. Give them a good story that evokes emotion and compels them to act. And give them a strong call to action that spells out exactly what you want them to do. When you pay attention to these steps and keep your readers in mind, you can learn to write

right-sell now.

Did You Like What You Read?

If you liked this book, or found it helpful in any way, please head over to Amazon and post a review. All you need to do is go to Amazon, search for the book, and leave your thoughts.

It would mean a lot to me, and it may just help someone else find it.

Acknowledgements

A special thanks to the people who have provided support and encouragement throughout my professional career, and writing this book.

Brian Basilico
Ellen Huxtable
Megan Langston
Laura Swalec
Jennifer Bowe
Meg Brennan
Pam Brennan
Jim Brennan

Thank you to all the people who read and gave their input on early drafts. It helped!

About The Author

Matt Brennan is a Chicago-area copywriter who has helped hundreds of businesses tell stories that sell since 2009. He specializes in blogging, website content, press releases, and other forms of marketing writing. He's helped publicly traded companies, school districts, and small to medium-sized businesses with their marketing goals. In addition to his client work, he writes about blogging and content marketing at

matthewlbrennan.com. His marketing

writing has also appeared on high profile

industry websites, such as ProBlogger,

Business2Community, and

Addicted2Success.

Matt is a former journalist, published in

Boys' Life, the Chicago Sun-Times, and

several local magazines and newspapers.

He loves feature writing and storytelling,

and transferring those skill sets to the

business community.

When Matt is not working he is probably

spending time with his lovely wife, Meg,

3-year-old son, Jamie, and German

shepherd mix, Captain. He may be writing about whatever whacky thing his son did next, at SpiralingUpwards.com. He loves loud music, and despite his best interests, he is obsessed with the Cubs and Bears.

Want to say hi? Drop me a line at matt@matthewlbrennan.com.

www.ingramcontent.com/pod-product-compliance
Lightning Source LLC
Chambersburg PA
CBHW070252190526
45169CB00001B/381